Garden Projects

in a weekend

Garden Projects

in a weekend

Julie London

JOURNEY EDITIONS
Boston • Tokyo

Acknowledgments

Thanks to everyone who has worked on this book – a testament to team effort.

First published in the United States in 2000 by Journey Editions, an imprint of Periplus Editions (HK) Ltd, with editorial offices at 153 Milk Street, Boston, Massachusetts 02109.

Copyright © 2000 Merehurst Limited
Originally published by Merehurst Limited in 1998.

ISBN: 1-58290-017-5

Distributed in the U.S. by
TUTTLE PUBLISHING
DISTRIBUTION CENTER
Airport Industrial Park
364 Innovation Drive
North Clarendon, VT 05759-9436
Tel: (800) 526-2778
Tel: (802) 773-8930

Printed in Hong Kong
First U.S. edition
06 05 04 03 02 01 00
10 9 8 7 6 5 4 3 2 1

Contents

Introduction *6*

Games table *8*

Copper arbor *12*

Night lights *18*

Etagère *22*

Bird house *28*

Hanging basket *34*

Pallet sun lounger *38*

Stepping stones *44*

Tablecloth *50*

Children's wigwam *54*

Wire frame for climbing plants *58*

Canopy *62*

Mosaic pond *66*

Decking *72*

Glossary *76*

Suppliers *79*

Index *80*

Introduction

How many times have you seen magazines featuring beautifully photographed pictures of gardens with lovely ideas for furniture and interesting focal points and thought, if only I could make that? Well, here is the book that will help you do just that, giving you inspiring and achievable ideas with which to furnish your garden.

Many of the projects are suitable for small gardens or balconies, or they can be adapted for small spaces. For instance, if you do not have a large garden, the canopy on page 62 can be made smaller and adapted into a sort of veranda by screwing the eyes into the brickwork of the house and placing two poles opposite them in the garden. The bird house, hanging basket and wire frame for climbing plants will fit in very small spaces, and even the mosaic pond can be scaled down in size to sit in a corner of a balcony.

I have tried to use materials that are easily available and things that you might usually throw away. The pallet sun lounger and night lights are prime examples of using discarded materials that can be given new life with a bit of imagination. The tools I have used are those you would probably have anyway if you do a bit of DIY, or at least you should be able to borrow them quite easily from friends and family.

The restful qualities of a garden cannot be overestimated. The smallest plot can be decorated with pots and trellises, and perhaps a bird house. All can add color to the existing planting scheme, and paint, mosaics and stencilling will give extra interest to a garden when plants die down and are between growing seasons.

You do not even have to be an avid gardener to appreciate the merits of decorating your garden. The current trend for extending the house into the garden, in effect adding an outside room to your home, also brings lots of design opportunities. It helps to feel confident when attempting these projects, so start with a small simple one, such as the painted-jar night lights; the end product belies the simplicity of this project. Then progress up to the larger projects. The most complicated one is the copper arbor; you will need someone to help you make this and probably all the larger items. An important point to remember is to use the right tools for the job; it takes most of the

frustration out of making things – although not all of it.

It is crucial that you use the right materials. For instance, if you skimp and use ordinary tile adhesive and grout on the mosaic pond, instead of swimming-pool adhesive and waterproof grout, the pond may not be watertight. Also, these specialist products are formulated to withstand extremes of temperature, which is imperative for a pond that will be left outside all year round. However, where possible or relevant I have used basic readily available materials.

The idea of this book is to inspire you to do your own thing, use bright colors in the garden, innovate your own designs and to use this as a starting point to further your creative ideas. We all had great fun working on this book, and I hope you have fun making the projects. Enjoy the summer and the fruits of your labor.

Games table

It is hard to believe that this table started life as a door. Customize it to your own design incorporating a chess and checkers board to while away summer afternoons.

Planning your time

DAY ONE
AM: Buy your materials and cut to size

PM: Attach and paint the legs; prime the top

DAY TWO
AM: Sponge checkerboard; paint design

PM: Apply varnish

Tools and materials

Hollow core door, 28 in (70 cm) wide

1½ x 1½ in (35 x 35 mm) softwood

16 right-angle brackets

Pencil

Screws

Vice

Paint and primer

Sponges

Jigsaw

Drill

Exterior varnish

I nspired by the outdoor tradition of playing chess, cards and backgammon, this games table for all ages makes a lovely addition to the summer garden. The chessboard pattern is easy to paint; I simply sponged it on using sponges cut from the packing for wine glasses. Use two shades of the same color so that the pattern is obviously a chessboard, but let your imagination loose when designing the rest of the table.

Hollow core doors are available from building supply companies. You need to buy a flush door with no panelling or you will have difficulty painting it. Cut the blank to size and patch the end that is cut, or just paint over it. The legs of the table are made from the thickest square softwood that I could obtain and are fixed on with right-angle brackets. You could even make the table from suitable discarded materials.

The whole table was painted in household latex paint (watered down a bit to make it more manageable) on top of a coat of primer paint. I gave it an ethnic feel by painting curls and spots in bright colors. The edges of the table were sponged to match the chessboard in the center.

You could also try painting a backgammon board or chutes and ladders, or perhaps use blackboard paint for scoreboards on the corners. The possibilities are endless. If you feel uncomfortable painting a freehand design, try stencilling, or even découpage. Then just give the table a few coats of exterior varnish to protect it. It is advisable to bring the table inside during the winter.

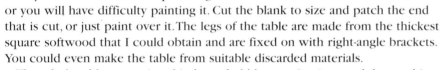

Day One

Step 1
Cut the door down to 4 ft
(120 cm) in length. Cut four pieces of
softwood for the legs to 30 in (73 cm)
in length.

Step 2
Mark the position of the legs on the
underside of the table. Do this by
standing each of the legs upright,
positioning the right-angle brackets on
the edge of the table and marking
through the holes on the table and the
leg with a pencil.

Step 3
Place the leg in the vice and screw the
brackets onto the legs, following the
pencil marks. You will need to stagger
the position of the screws or they may
meet in the middle of the leg.

Step 4
Screw the legs onto the table as shown
in the photograph.

Step 5
Paint the legs *in situ* using household
latex paint. I painted the legs different
colors, but you may prefer to paint
them all the same color. Paint over the
brackets and give the legs at least two
coats of paint.

Saving on paint

Paint your design with ordinary leftover
household latex paint or acrylic craft
paint. This will save you from buying large
cans of color that you may not use again.

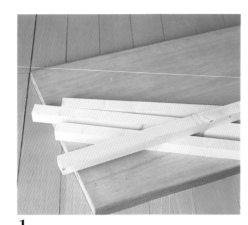

1

2

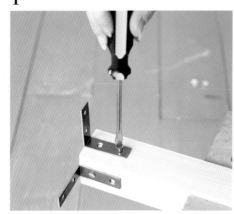

3

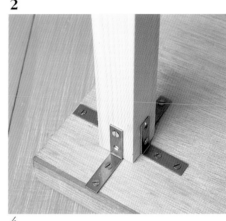

4

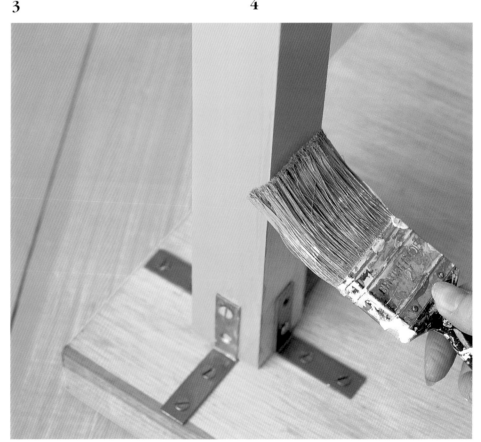

5

6

Step 6
Turn the table over and give the top and sides a coat of primer. This makes the top easier to work on when drawing a freehand design.

Day Two

Step 7
To make the squares of the checkerboard, cut two 2 in (5 cm) squares of sponge. The piece of sponge I used came from the packing for a set of glasses.

Step 8
Mark the center position of the table with a cross, using a ruler to get the lines straight. All the squares will radiate from this central position.

Step 9
Sponge four center squares using two different colors, diagonally opposite each other. Continue sponging until you have eight squares across and eight squares top to bottom, radiating from the four center squares.

Step 10
I painted a further pattern around the checkerboard with an elliptical, slightly Mexican-inspired design in orange and mauve, with swirls of green, highlighted with yellow and white dots. Two coats of exterior varnish will help it to withstand the weather.

7

8

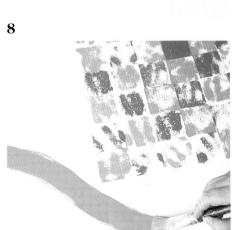

9

10

Copper arbor

This whimsical arbor makes a wonderful focal point in a garden. Covered in sweet-smelling roses or jasmine, the arbor is somewhere to sit and contemplate – a tiny paradise in itself.

Planning your time

DAY ONE
AM: Buy your materials
PM: Make former; bend pipes; make dome
DAY TWO
AM: Hammer in stakes, attach dome
PM: Attach crossrails

Tools and materials

Five 3 yd (3 m) lengths of ⅝ in (15 mm) diameter copper piping

Six 6 ft (183 cm) rounded and pointed garden stakes

⅝ in (15 mm) flat wood drill bit

Sheet of medium density fiberboard at least 3 ft (1 m) wide to make former

String and pencil

Vice

⅝ in (15 mm) spring former

¼ in (6 mm) drill bit

¼ in (6 mm) nut

Junior hacksaw

Wood scraps

Hammer

Mallet

The most difficult part in making this arbor is curving the pipes without flattening them. In order to do this you will have to make a template; there is really no other way of doing it. You will also need someone to give you a hand throughout this project because it is a large item to construct.

The copper pipes are the type that are used for plumbing and can be bought singly or in bundles of ten; you will need about five for the arbor. With age, and exposed to the elements, the copper will oxidize and take on an attractive green patina.

Once the pipes have been bent and the centers flattened, the flattened parts of the pipes will be weak and brittle until they are fixed together, so be careful when you are handling them.

The uprights are made from normal garden stakes obtained from a garden center. I bought ready-treated ones and hammered them straight into the ground with a mallet, using a carpenter's level to make sure they were straight. The horizontal cross-pipes to brace the arbor were put in on site, to get them as accurate as possible.

The arbor is designed so that you can grow sweet-smelling vines up the stakes and around the pipes, but it looks just as handsome without plants. Large pots around the base give the arbor more visual substance.

A candle or outdoor light suspended from the center will cast a gentle glow in the early evening, and an unusual adornment, such as a mobile, will please the eye. Use your arbor as a welcome retreat at the end of the day.

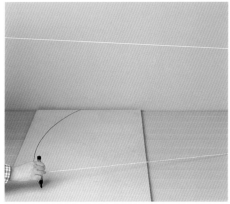

1

Day One

Step 1

First, make an arc on which to bend the pipes without flattening them. Take a 3 ft (1 m) piece of string tied to a pencil or pen at one end, and staple or nail the other end to the floor. Then draw an arc on a sheet of MDF, or scrap wood, which is at least 3 ft (1 m) wide.

Step 2

Cut out the arc with a jigsaw.

Step 3

Put the arc in a vice and bend the copper piping, starting at one end and gradually working along the length of each piece. Do not try to bend the piping in one attempt or it will slip off the arc. You will need someone to help you do this.

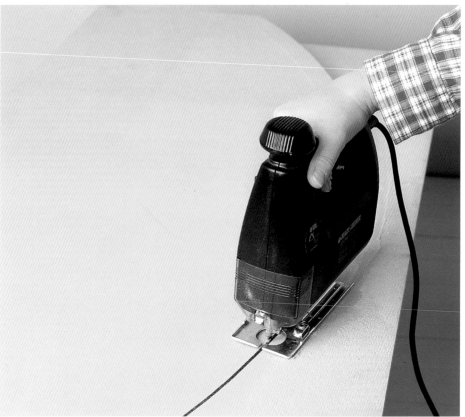

2

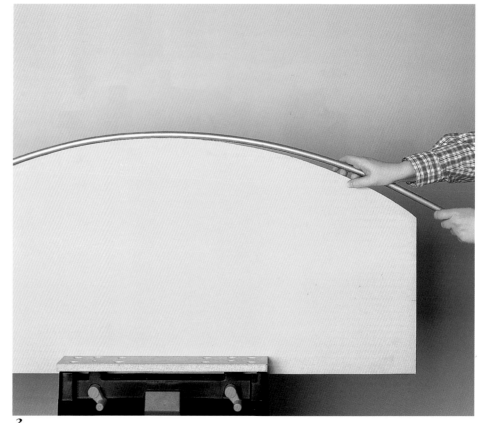

3

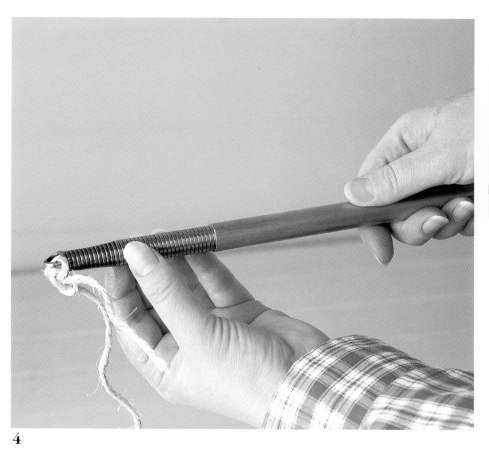

4

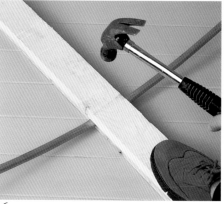

6

5

Step 4

To bend the ends of the pipe at an angle without flattening them, insert a ⅝ in (15 mm) spring former in each end, attaching a piece of string to the spring so that you can get it out easily afterwards. Some oil on the spring will make it easier to get in and out; cooking oil will do.

Step 5

Put the ends of the piping in a vice up to 2 in (5 cm) and bend the pipe until it is at an angle; ask your helper to hold the vice still if it is not screwed to an immovable surface.

Step 6

Find the central point of each tube and mark with masking tape. Sandwich the pipe between two pieces of wood offcuts and hammer the center flat.

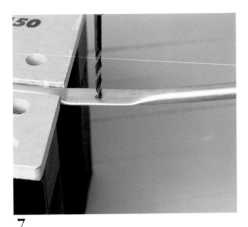

7

8

Step 7

Put the pipe in the vice again, ask someone to hold the end steady, and drill a hole through the center of the flattened part. Do this with a ¼ in (6 mm) drill bit.

Step 8

Join the three arcs of tubing with the nut through the holes you have just drilled, as shown in the photograph.

Step 9

Drill a hole in the middle of the top of each post with a ⅝ in (15 mm) flat wood drill bit, deep enough to hold the copper pipes.

Drilling the posts

The holes that are drilled in the top of each post need to be slightly larger than the diameter of the pipes in order to alleviate pressure on the arcs when they are being put into the top of the posts. The tightened nut will keep them stable once they are in place.

9

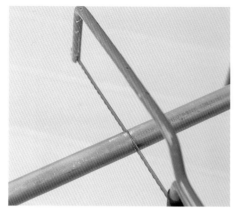

10

Day Two

Step 10

To determine the position of the stakes, place the copper dome on the ground and mark the six points where it sits on the ground. Undo the arcs as they will be difficult to insert into the tops of the stakes and may break at the point where they are flattened.

Hammer the stakes into the ground with a mallet on the inside of the marks you have made on the ground for the dome. This is a two-person job; one standing on a ladder to hammer, and the other to make sure the stakes are straight. Put the copper arcs back up, reattaching them with the nut through the center.

To make the crossrails measure the distance between each stake, cut a length of copper pipe to bridge this distance plus an extra ¾ in (2 cm).

Step 11

Drill a hole 2 in (5 cm) from the top of either side of each stake with the ⅝ in (15 mm) drill bit, to take the copper crossrails that you have just cut. Position the holes towards the inside of each stake.

Step 12

The photograph shows how the configuration of the pipes and stakes works. Now all that remains is to plant some vines.

11

12

Night lights

Punching tins and painting jars are practical ways of making something from nothing and an economical way of lighting the garden in the summer, especially if you need lots of lights.

Planning your time

DAY ONE
AM: Prepare tin cans; make tracing

PM: Drill holes in tins; paint, string and place in garden

DAY TWO
AM: Prepare glass jars and paint them

PM: Place in garden

Tools and materials

A selection of tins (fruit, tomatoes, beans etc.)

Glass jars

Drill

Vice

Tracing paper

Masking tape

Glass paints

Resist outliner

Wire

Night lights

Can opener

Paint Thinner

Use any tin cans – fruit, tomato, baked beans – and take the tops off using an opener that leaves the thicker rim on. The rim gives the tin a bit of stability, and you will have a jagged edge otherwise. Make sure the tins are clean inside. The tins are punched using a drill either in a random design or one that is traced onto paper. Use a vice, or something to hold the tins, as the drill bit may slip when you are drilling on the shiny metal surface. The tins are painted with glass paints, and take on a Mexican feel when strung together.

Small glass jars also make effective night lights. When tinted with glass paints, available from art suppliers, they glow with the color of the paint. Draw a design with a resist outliner, and color in the design with paint, or draw abstract shapes on top of a layer of color. Follow the contours of the jars and tins to make painting the design easier.

When it comes to lighting up, use night lights in their own aluminium cases inside, as the tins and glass will be too hot to handle and the jars may crack with excess heat.

You can customize tins and jars for outside parties, lighting a path to a doorway, or hang them in trees. However you use them, they will add a magical quality to any occasion.

1

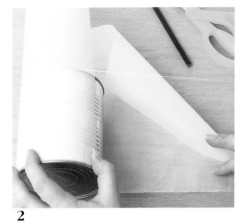

2

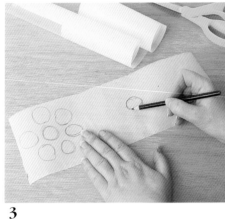

3

Tin can night lights

Step 1
Remove the labels and take the tops off the tin cans with an opener that leaves the thicker rim intact, otherwise you may cut yourself on the edge.

Step 2
Wrap the tin can in tracing paper, then cut the paper to the size of the tin.

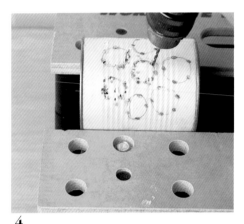

4

5

Step 3
Draw your design on the tracing paper, keeping it very simple or it will be too difficult to drill. Mark dots at intervals along the outline of the pattern.

Step 4
Stick the tracing paper around the can with masking tape. Place the tin in a vice to hold it steady while you drill. Using a small drill bit, drill holes through the can along the dots marked on the pattern.

Step 5
Paint the cans with glass paints. The daisy on this design was picked out in different colors.

Step 6
Thread fine wire through opposite holes at the top of the can. Place a night light in the bottom, light with a taper, and hang in a safe place in the garden.

6

1

Glass jar night lights

Step 1

To make the jar night lights, first wash the glass jars thoroughly, soaking off all the labels in a bowl of hot soapy water.

Step 2

Use paint thinner to remove any stubborn sticky glue that remains. Make sure the jar is completely dry, then apply your base color using glass paint. Apply further coats when dry. Glass paint is translucent – the more coats you give the jars, the deeper the color will be.

Step 3

When the base color is dry, apply your own freehand design with a resist outliner, all around the jar.

Step 4

Wrap wire around the neck of the jar, twisting it around itself to secure it, then loop it over the top of the jar and anchor it as shown in the photograph. Twist the excess wire around the loop. Put a night light in the jar, light with a long taper and hang in a safe place in the garden.

2

3

4

Etagère

Avid gardeners will appreciate having somewhere to keep their pots and tools together. This made-to-measure staging can be customized for even the smallest garden.

This étagère is a cross between plant staging and a work station. Made from rough-sawn lumber for the garden, it would also sit well in a conservatory or hallway if that is the only space you have available.

The two-tier design gives you enough storage space for tall pots, a slot for garden stakes and pitch fork and shovel. The top rail has copper nails from which to hang jute, trowels and wire, and there is space underneath for seed trays and spare pots.

I made this étagère to measure 5 ft (1.5 meters) wide by 5 ft (1.5 metres) high, but of course you can make yours to any size to fit the space available for it. It can be used to bring height to the garden, and if you change the pots for each season you could have a garden in constant flower. Several of these, overflowing with flowers in bloom, would make a huge impact.

I painted the étagère with a fashionable blue water-based stain that is harmless to plants, to bring it to life. You could just as easily use leftover latex paint but, of course, it would not wear as well, although there is nothing to prevent you painting it different colors in subsequent years.

Planning your time

DAY ONE

AM: Buy materials; cut wood to size

PM: Make three main frames; screw on slats

DAY TWO

AM: Screw on back rails and crossbraces

PM: Paint on wood stain

Tools and materials

2 x 1 in (50 x 25 mm) sawn lumber

2¾ x 1 in (70 x 25 mm) sawn lumber

Screws

Countersinking tool

Nails

Right angle

Copper common nails

Jigsaw

PVA glue

Wood stain

Day One

Step 1

Cut three lengths of 2 x 1 in (50 x 25 mm) lumber to 60 in (150 cm) long for the back legs. Divide them into 20 in (50 cm) lengths, which determines the spacing of the shelves. Use a right angle to get the lines straight. Put them to one side.

Cut three more lengths of 2 x 1 in (50 x 25 mm) lumber to 22 in (55 cm) for the supports for the bottom shelf and measure 8 in (20 cm) from one end on each piece.

Step 2

Cut three more lengths of 2 x 1 in (50 x 25 mm) lumber to 21½ in (55 cm) and mark two staggered holes at the end of each piece and drill pilot holes. These pieces form the front middle legs.

Step 3

Apply waterproof PVA glue around the holes for an extra firm hold.

Step 4

Secure the middle legs with screws to the support for the bottom shelf inside the 8 in (20 cm) line.

Step 5

Use the right angle to make sure the middle legs are straight and secure with the second screw. You now have a T-section.

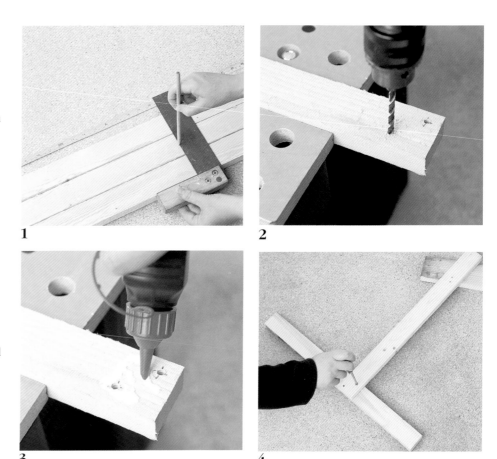

1

2

3

4

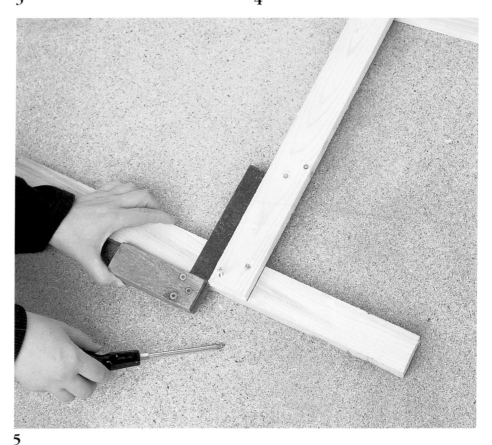

5

6

7

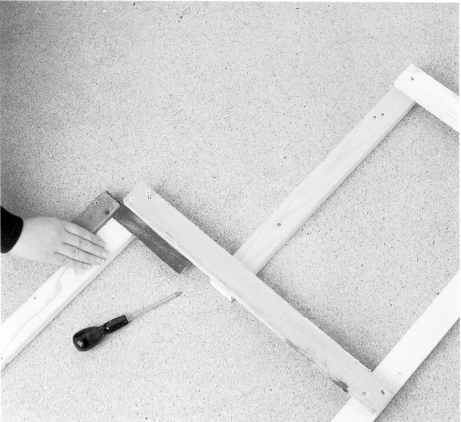

8

Step 6
Flip the T-section over and screw it to the inside of one of the back legs inside the first 20 in (50 cm) line.

Step 7
Cut three 14 in (35 cm) lengths of 2 x 1 in (50 x 25 mm) lumber. Screw one to the inside of the "T" and inside the second 20 in (50 cm) line marked on the back leg.

Step 8
Check all the right angles with a right angle so that the étagère will stand up straight when it is finished.

Step 9
Make two more of these frames in the same way, so that you have three – two ends and a middle. The supports for the shelves should all be on the inside of the frames.

9

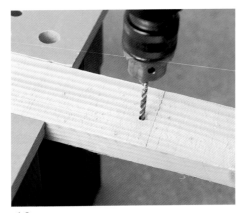

10

11

12

Step 10

To make the shelves, cut seven pieces of 2¾ x 1 in (70 x 25 mm) lumber to 60 in (150 cm) each and one to 30 in (75 cm). Draw the center line across all the 60 in (150 cm) pieces of lumber and drill a hole to the left of each line and at each end. The top shelf will have three slats and the bottom will have four long slats and one short one.

Step 11

Mark the position of the slats across the depth of the bottom shelf support so that they are evenly spaced.

Step 12

Screw the lumber to the top and bottom shelf supports.

Step 13

This is how the bottom shelf should look. The gap on the right is to stand stakes, brooms and other tall objects.

13

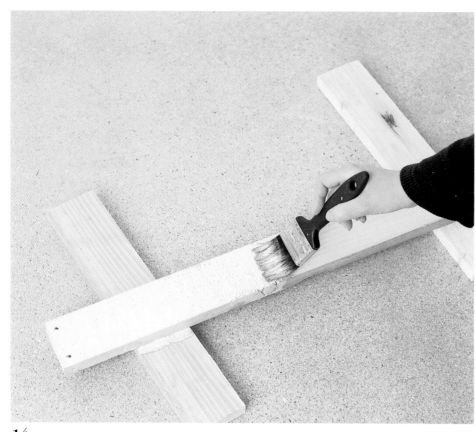

14

16

Day Two

Step 14
Cut three pieces of wood to size for the back rails and drill pilot holes to screw them to the main frame. Paint with wood stain.

Step 15
Hammer in copper nails to hang raffia, wire and garden tools onto what will be the top rail.

Step 16
Screw the back rails onto the front of the main frame. To brace the back, mark a piece of 2¾ x 1 in (70 x 25 mm) wood as shown, from the top left corner to the point where the bottom shelf meets the center upright. Cut down with a jigsaw and screw it to the back. Do the same for the other side, giving you a "V" shape. Paint the whole étagère with wood stain to protect it.

15

Bird house

A colorful accessory for the garden, this bird house is a working model and in time should attract wildlife to your garden, once the birds get used to its decoration.

These bird houses are designed to attract small birds as well as to make a decorative feature in the garden. Small holes that are common in old trees are usually in short supply in a small garden, so a bird house like this should attract birds to nest in your garden. Chickadees usually visit a bird box soon after it has been put up, so make the center hole no bigger than 1⅛ in (29 mm) in diameter, or the nesting box may be colonized by bigger birds such as starlings.

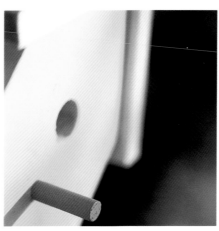

The join at the peak of the roof is sealed with waterproof glue, and there are drainage holes in the floor of the box. The front can also be removed so that the inside can be cleaned out after the birds have gone. Use brass or galvanized screws for the front of the house as they will not rust.

The two bird houses shown here were painted with leftover latex paint, to make them a decorative feature in the garden. You could also use colored wood stains for a more woody look if you prefer, or even just leave your bird house unpainted, but with a coat of varnish to protect it.

I am sure you will derive a lot of pleasure from watching the birds in your garden, or balcony – you will be amazed at just how much time you can enjoyably while away!

1

Day One

Step 1

To make the front of the bird house, cut a piece of 6 x ¾ in (150 x 20 mm) softwood to a length of 10 in (250 mm). Find the center point at the top, angle both sides so that they match as shown in the photograph and cut out with a jigsaw to make the pitch of the roof. Use this piece as a template for the back, drawing around the pitch so that you get two identical pieces.

Step 2

You will need to make the sides narrower than the front and back, so that the roof fits on neatly. Deduct the thickness of the front and back (1½ in [40 mm]) from the width of the pine. Cut out with a jigsaw.

Step 3

To obtain the correct height for the sides, place the piece of softwood you have just cut next to the front piece and mark the point where the pitch meets this piece. Cut two pieces of wood this size.

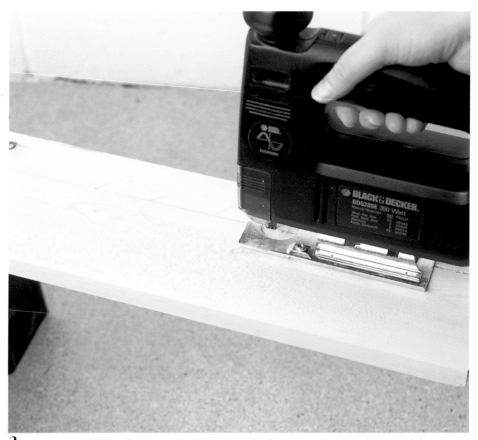

2

3

Step 4

The floor of the bird house sits inside the walls so you need to measure inside the walls. Cut out a piece of wood to this measurement. You should now have a front and a back piece that are the same, two sides and a floor.

Step 5

Screw the back to the sides as shown in the photograph, using the floor to keep the pieces square. Glue them together first.

Step 6

Nail the bottom of the sides to the floor, having glued them first.

Step 7

The roof is made from the same wood as the front and back and is therefore the same width. To make sure the two pieces of the roof meet neatly at the apex, set the jigsaw blade at the same angle as the pitch of the roof. Do this by holding the blade on the line of the apex and moving the base plate until it is at the same angle as the slope of the side. You might need someone to help you do this.

Step 8

Cut two pieces of roof just a little longer than the inner pitch of the roof to make a peak, so that the falling rain clears the bird house.

Using a jigsaw

Most jigsaws come with a movable base plate. This allows you to cut wood at an angle by unscrewing the base plate and aligning it with the angle you want to cut.

4

5

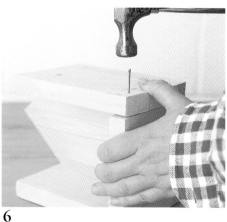

6

7

8

9

10

11

Day Two

Step 9

Drill a hole in the front for the entrance, just above the center, using a 1 in (25 mm) flat wood drill bit. Drill a smaller hole below this for the perch, using a ½ in (10 mm) flat wood drill bit.

Step 10

Cut a 2½ in (60 mm) length of ½ in (10 mm) dowelling and glue it into the smaller hole. Drill a hole in the back piece, to hang the bird house on a nail.

Step 11

Screw the front of the bird house onto the sides. Pre-drill the holes in the front and use brass or galvanized screws, as they will not rust.

Step 12

To make the roof, glue the two angles together using PVA glue, for the peak.

12

13

15

16

14

Step 13
Put the roof on the bird house and nail it to the back.

Step 14
Nail the two sides of the roof together with panel pins and seal with a line of PVA glue to make the join watertight.

Step 15
Drill drainage holes in the base to let any water drain out and allow air to circulate.

Step 16
Apply two coats of paint to the bird house, hang it in the garden and enjoy the wildlife that may nest there.

Hanging basket

Although store-bought baskets are not expensive, making your own gives you the opportunity to have a unique design, made from materials you already have at home.

Most hanging baskets are made from wire, and this one is no different, except that it is completely personalized. It is a way of showing off all those shells, pebbles and bits of driftwood that you pick up on the beach.

The basic shape of the basket looks more like a wastebasket, but when it is planted up, it looks beautiful. I planted the one shown here with sweet alyssum, portaluca and scaveola, but of course you can plant yours with your own favorite flowering plants. Simple S hooks, available from hardware stores, are ideal for hanging baskets from a bracket and attaching chains.

To prevent the compost from drying out, use a thickish plastic bag to line the inside, between the moss and compost; you can buy the moss at most garden centers. Use a container compost because it is better for the plants, and it is a good idea to add some slow-release fertilizer and water-retaining pellets.

Wire in pebbles and shells so they hang from the bottom of the basket. You could also try glass beads, pieces of cutlery or anything interesting that will catch the light.

Planning your time

DAY ONE
AM: Assemble the components; cut chicken wire; attach circles and base

PM: Wire in pebbles, shells, driftwood etc.

DAY TWO
AM: Plant up the basket

PM: Hang basket from bracket

Tools and materials

⅛ in (2 mm) galvanized wire

1/16 in (1 mm) galvanized wire for tying

Chicken wire

4 S hooks

3 lengths of chain

Whole sphagnum moss

Plastic bag as a liner

Potting soil

Wire cutters

Round-nosed pliers

1

Day One

Step 1
Make three circles, decreasing in size, with lengths of ⅛ in (2 mm) galvanized wire, wiring the ends together with ¹⁄₁₆ in (1 mm) wire.

Step 2
Cut a piece of chicken wire to the circumference of the largest circle by required depth of the basket.

Step 3
Bend the top edge of the chicken wire over the largest circle and secure with ¹⁄₁₆ in (1 mm) wire.

Making extra circles
Use long lengths of wire to make smaller circles, coiling the wire together to give it extra strength.

2

3

Step 4

Place the second circle of wire around the middle of the basket, securing it with ⅟₁₆ in (1 mm) wire. The chicken wire will fold into a natural cone shape. Mould the base to roughly the same size as the smallest circle.

Step 5

Cut a circle of chicken wire a bit bigger than the circumference of the base and fold the edges over the edge of the smallest wire circle.

Step 6

Fix the circle of chicken wire to the main body of the basket by looping the ⅟₁₆ in (1 mm) wire through the holes in the chicken wire and then twisting the ends together.

Step 7

Wire pebbles and pieces of driftwood to the outside of the main frame with ⅟₁₆ in (1 mm) wire and a pair of round-nosed pliers. Wire bits around the base so that they hang down when the basket is hung from a bracket.

Day Two

Step 8

Line the hanging basket with moss. Cut a thick plastic bag to fit between the moss and the compost and fill up with compost. Cut holes in the side of the basket and the plastic to insert the plants, taking care not to scratch yourself on the cut wire. Attach three S hooks to the sides, then the chains and use one S hook to hold all three chains together and to hang from a bracket.

Note: Sphagnum moss is available as "whole" and "milled." The latter is finely ground and used as a seed starter. Be sure to purchase "whole" moss; otherwise, it will sift through the holes of the chicken wire.

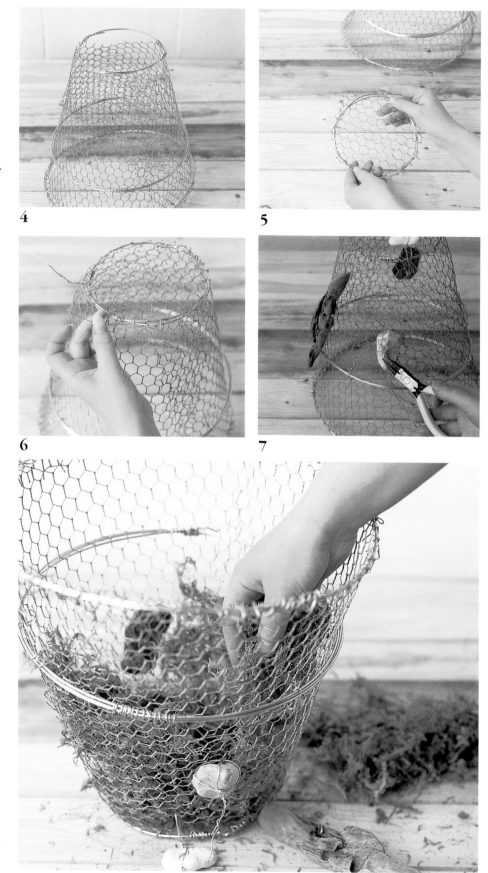

4

5

6

7

8

Pallet sun lounger

Cast-off builders' pallets are ideal for relaxing on in the garden, with a simple foam mattress for comfort, so you can while away the hours in the shade of a tree.

Planning your time

DAY ONE
AM: Acquire two pallets of the same size. Buy other materials

PM: Make the base cushions

DAY TWO
AM: Make the bolster cover

PM: Put the lounger in the garden, lie in the sun and relax

Tools and materials

2 wooden pallets the same size

2 pieces of 2 in (5 cm) thick foam cut to fit

1 store-bought bolster cushion

Fabric to cover foam and bolster

Fusible web

Small eyelets and eyelet punch

String

T he beauty of this idea is that it makes use of something that is usually thrown away. Most building supply companies have non-returnable pallets that are usually discarded, though you may have to pay a token amount for them – square it with the man on the gate before you help yourself. Make sure you pick up two pallets that are the same size, as they do vary.

Two blocks of foam cut to size, from an upholsterers' shop or fabric store, will make substantial mattresses. The foam will probably be the most expensive item to buy, since all foam is now treated with a fire retardant. The bolster, which provides support for your head, is store bought, but in its place you could use an old rolled-up bath towel or a cushion to give the same effect.

This project involves no sewing at all. The fabric covers are held in place with eyelets and laces, and all the raw edges are hemmed with fusible web, including the bolster, so there is no need for a sewing machine.

The pallets can be split up and used as individual seating for summer barbecues if you have lots of guests.

1

Day One

Step 1
The pallets may need cleaning up a bit as they will probably have been lying around outside for a while. Sand away any splinters from the edges that might catch on clothes.

Step 2
Have two pieces of foam cut to just a bit smaller than each pallet – about ¾ in (2 cm) smaller all round will be enough.

Step 3
To make covers for the foam, wrap the fabric around the sides as shown in the photograph. Use enough fabric to leave 8 in (20 cm) or so over at the top and bottom, 16 in (40 cm) in total.

2

3

4

6

5

Step 4

Hem the top and bottom edges with fusible web, using a hot iron and following the manufacturer's instructions. Turn under a ¾ in (2 cm) hem as you go along. The sides will not need turning under as the selvedge will stop the fabric fraying.

Step 5

Turn the top and bottom of the fabric onto the underside of the foam.

Step 6

Measure the spacing for the eyelets along the sides of the fabric, about every 8 in (20 cm). Mark the positions with a pin.

Joining seams without sewing

If you do not have access to a sewing machine, join seams and turn under hems with a strip of fusible web. All you need is a hot iron and a clean cloth to protect your fabric.

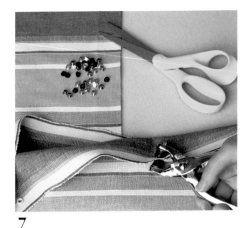

7

Step 7

Insert the eyelets where marked using an eyelet punch.

Step 8

Lace the fabric through the eyelets to keep it in place.

Day Two

Step 9

To measure the cover for the bolster wrap the fabric round it, with a ½ in (1.5 cm) excess so that it is not too tight. Use the full width of the fabric.

8

9

Using eyelets
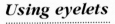

Eyelets are a quick and useful way to decorate fabrics. Here they have been used for fixing the cover to a foam base. This makes the cover easy to remove for washing and saves on fabric.

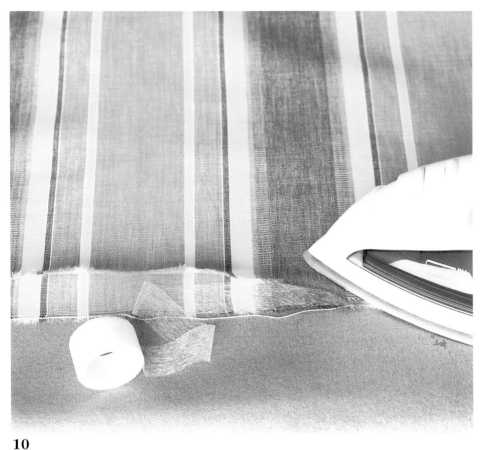

10

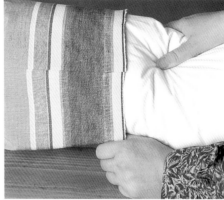

12

13

11

Step 10
Place the two cut sides of the bolster cover right sides together and join them with fusible web, using a hot iron and following the manufacturer's instructions.

Step 11
Fold the seam back on itself so that it lies flat when turned the right way round.

Step 12
Turn the cover right side out and pull it over the bolster, positioning the bolster in the middle of the cover.

Step 13
Place the bolster on the lounger and arrange the excess fabric so that it drapes over the edge on each side. You might want an extra cushion for comfort when you are reading.

Stepping stones

Making a paving slab is a lot easier than you might think. These ones are functional as well as decorative – the opportunity to use decoration in the garden is always welcome.

Planning your time

DAY ONE
AM: Buy your materials; make the frames

PM: Make concrete and indent shapes

DAY TWO
AM: Take the paving stones out of the frames

PM: Lay them in the garden

Tools and materials

A bag of white cement

½ in (10 mm) gravel

Builders' sand

Concrete colorant

Pine battens 4 x 4 in (100 x 100 mm)

Electric drill

Screws

Trowel

Cooking oil

Paintbrush

Lead-free solder

Sheet of plastic

You will have to make these paving slabs in a day as they need to be left to dry overnight. This idea enables you to make a feature of the stones, so that you can slot them into existing paving. They can be placed as stepping stones across a lawn, or in a gravelled area with ground-hugging plants.

Decorate them with abstract curves of wire, as I have, or make mosaic patterns with broken pieces of china. Try impressing leaves or decorative tiles into each slab.

These stepping stones can be made to whatever size you want. I made mine 12 in (30 cm) square, but they are heavy once dry, so do not make them too large. If you are making more than one stone, make all the frames first. Increase the quantities of sand, aggregate and cement, but always keep them in the same proportions. Use a uniform measure, such as a cut-down plastic drinks bottle as I have used here.

White cement will ensure the color is as pure as possible. It is more expensive than grey cement but not prohibitively so. If you do use the standard grey color, however, expect the final color of your slabs to be affected; it will be a bit murkier. Concrete colorant comes in about six colors, depending on the manufacturer, and you can buy it in a hardware store. It is not sold as a DIY product, but you should have no trouble obtaining it.

1

Day One

Step 1

To make the frame for a 12 in (30 cm) square paving stone, cut four lengths of softwood 12¾ in (32 cm) long. Place them at right angles and mark the depth of the batten at right angles (¾ in [2 cm]) against one edge of each of the battens.

Step 2

Drill screw holes through each batten, inside the ¾ in (2 cm) lines that you have just marked.

Step 3

Place the batten in a vice and screw the battens together, at right angles, through the holes that you drilled into the end of the adjacent batten.

Making reusable battens

The battens can be reused if they are screwed together through the end grain of the wood rather than glued or nailed together. If they are screwed it also makes it easier to remove the stepping stones when they have dried.

2

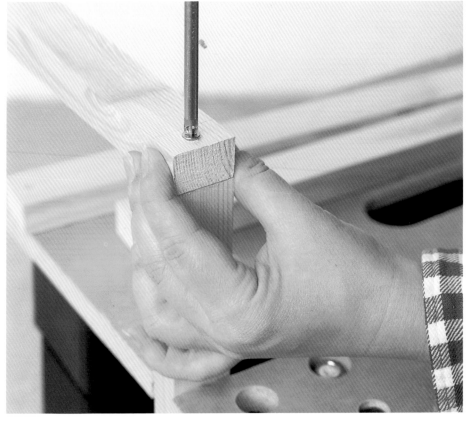

3

4

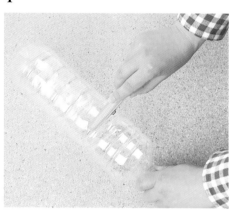

5

6

Step 4
Fit all the battens together to make a square frame.

Step 5
Make a measure for the ingredients from a plastic water bottle. Cut off the top part and use the bottom part as a guide for measuring the quantities.

Step 6
Make a halfway mark on the plastic bottle. Then measure out the quantities of ingredients thus: 1 part white cement; 2.5 parts aggregate (gravel); 2 parts sand; 0.5 colorant.

Step 7
Arrange the ingredients as shown in the photograph. First mix the sand and aggregate together with a trowel, next make a well in the middle, and put the cement in the well, then finally add your choice of colorant.

7

8

Step 8

Mix the cement and colorant together while still dry. Make a well in the middle and pour water into it, very slowly. Be careful not to fill the well too full and let the water spill over.

Step 9

Start mixing by folding the outside in with a trowel. Keep adding water until you get a workable consistency. Do not let the water escape, but keep it contained in the mixture. The mixture is ready when all the gravel is covered in color.

Step 10

Place the wooden frame on a sheet of plastic. Paint oil (cooking oil will do) around the inside edge of the frame and on the plastic within the frame to prevent the mixture sticking to the frame and plastic.

9

10

Step 11

Fill the frame with the mixture. Make sure it fills the frame completely, right into the corners and the edges.

Step 12

Smooth the top with a spare piece of wood, using a sawing and tapping action to make the gravel sink to the bottom and the cement rise to the top. There will be some indentations, but do not worry about these.

Step 13

Cut lengths of solder. Bend it into any shape you wish; it is very malleable. I made abstract swirls, which are easy to do and a pleasing shape to look at.

Step 14

Place the shapes in the cement. Press them down well so that they sit in the cement rather than on the top. If you get cement on the shapes wipe it off before it dries. Leave to dry overnight.

Day Two

Step 15

When the stone is dry, lift it from the plastic, and unscrew the frame at two corners. The frame should come away from the paving stone easily.

Lay out the paving stone in its position.

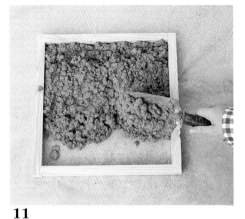

11

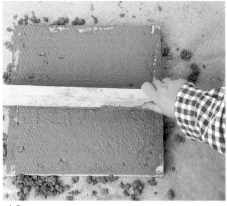

12

13

14

Making patterns in the stones

Lead-free solder, used by plumbers to seal pipes, is very pliable and easy to bend into shapes.

Alternatively, try using wire coat hangers to create the same effect, bending them with round-nosed pliers.

The stones can also be a canvas for creating mosaic pictures from pieces of broken china. Work out your pattern before you begin.

15

Tablecloth

A red and white check tablecloth brings a cheerful touch to dining al fresco. It is weighted down with stones found on the beach to prevent it blowing about in the wind.

Planning your time

DAY ONE
AM: Buy materials; cut out canvas

PM: Draw out grid; paint on color

DAY TWO
AM: Iron to seal color; draw on leaves

PM: Put in eyelets; hang stones

Tools and materials

350 g (12 oz) cotton duck canvas

Fabric paint

Paintbrush

Iron

Black felt-tip pen

Pencil

Tape measure

Fusible web

Eyelets

Eyelet cutting tool

Hammer

Stones

String

The inspiration for this tablecloth was taken from the traditional cloths used in Italian bistros. Made from mediumweight canvas, it is painted with fabric paint after first marking out a grid pattern. The fabric paint is watered down (six parts water to one part paint) to make it easier to use and so that it will go further. Also, you can create interesting shapes where two blocks of thinner color overlap.

This is a no-sew cloth. The edges are turned under with fusible web, or, for an even simpler method, you could fray the edges. Eyelets are hammered in on the corners so that you can hang weights to ensure the cloth will stay put in a strong wind.

This is an ideal opportunity to make use of all those beach finds. Stones with natural holes worn in them will keep the cloth still while you are eating on a breezy day; a string of shells is purely decorative, but gives the right feel. Alternatively, you could buy some heavy beads as embellishment.

To decorate the cloth I drew abstract leaves, with a fabric marker, to highlight the squares where the two lines cross. If you feel uncomfortable drawing freehand, you could stencil or stamp a design, or appliqué pieces of fabric using fusible web.

You can make this cloth to whatever size you want. Keep it in the car for when you come across one of those opportune picnic spots.

1

Day One

Step 1
Cut the canvas into a square. I did this by folding it diagonally, to make a triangle, then cut along the raw edge.

Step 2
Mark out squares every 4 in (10 cm) along the edges, joining them lightly with a pencil, to give you a guide for painting. Use a piece of wood to join the lines if the cloth is to be big.

Step 3
Water down the fabric paint in a glass jar, 1 part paint to 6 parts water, using the fabric paint container as a measure. Use a wide paintbrush to apply the paint in rough stripes. The paint will sit on the surface of the canvas to begin with, so you may need to work it in a bit with the brush.

2

Watering down fabric paint

Watering down fabric paint not only makes it go further, it also makes it easier to manage. On some fabrics it will give an attractive watery edge to the paint, similar to that of watercolor paint on paper.

3

Step 4

When you have finished one lot of vertical stripes, paint the rest at right angles to create a checked effect.

Day Two

Step 5

Seal the paint with a hot iron when it is dry following the paint manufacturer's instructions. Place a clean cloth over the tablecloth so as not to scorch it. Make sure you iron the whole tablecloth.

Step 6

Turn under a 1¼ in (3 cm) hem all the way round onto the wrong side of the tablecloth and press in place with fusible web to give a neat edge.

Step 7

Turn the tablecloth over, right side facing up. With a felt pen or fabric pen, outline the center squares where the two lines of paint cross; this does not have to be precise. Draw a freehand leaf in the center of each square.

Step 8

Put an eyelet in each corner of the tablecloth. Mark the position with a pencil and use the tool supplied with the eyelets to cut the hole. If the fabric is too thick, snip it away with a pair of scissors until the hole is big enough to take the eyelet.

Thread string or jute through the eyelet and hang a stone, large bead, or any small heavy object that will anchor the tablecloth in the wind.

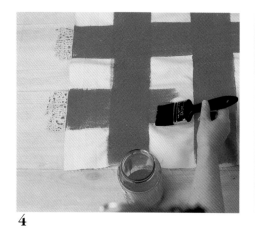

4

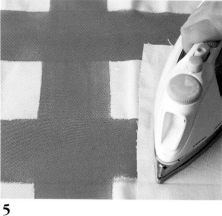

5

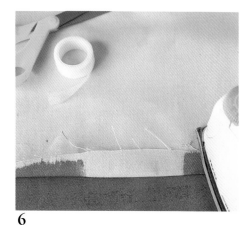

6

7

8

Children's wigwam

Made from simple materials, this delightful wigwam can be painted with ordinary household acrylic or fabric paint, and should keep children amused in the garden for hours.

Children love to make camps and dens, and to have special places of their own in which to hide and be secretive. This wigwam gives children a place to play and adds fuel to their imaginations. Once made, it can be put up in a jiffy.

The wigwam is made out of bamboo garden canes, which are available from garden centers, and a medium-weight canvas. The canvas can be painted with leftover household acrylic or fabric paint or can be decorated using felt pens. You could try making stamps from potatoes or sponges, making simple stencils, painting over leaves to leave a colored outline, or gluing on beads or pinning drawings to the wigwam.

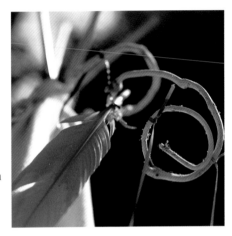

Depending on where you site the wigwam you might need to secure the legs into the grass. Although it was designed for play in the garden, it can also be put up indoors on a carpet.

Other alternatives are to make the wigwam from an old sheet, or sheeting which can be bought inexpensively by the yard. You could dye the fabric in the washing machine. It would also be fun to use fabric remnants, perhaps a different pattern for each panel. Broom handles could be used in place of the garden canes, but the wigwam will be much shorter.

Planning your time

DAY ONE
AM: Buy your materials

PM: Assemble stakes; cut out canvas; make opening

DAY TWO
AM: Sew sides and ties. Edge with ribbon

PM: Put together and paint

Tools and materials

Four 6 ft (2 m) garden stakes

4½ yd (4 m) of 12 oz (350 g) cotton duck canvas 172 in (83 cm) wide

Jute

Tape measure

Bias binding for ties

Ribbon for edging

Sewing machine

Fusible web

Day One

Step 1

Assemble the four garden stakes in a pyramid so that they are stable and tie them together with jute at the point where they all cross.

Step 2

Measure the distance between the four legs, making sure they are all equal. For the wigwam I made, the distance was 3 ft (1 m).

Step 3

Measure the distance between the poles about 2 in (5 cm) down from the point where the canes meet. In my wigwam it was about 2½ in (6 cm). Now measure the height of the canes to this point.

Step 4

Cut a rectangle of canvas; it needs to be a yard (3 ft) wide (plus ¾ in [2 cm] for the side seams), by the height of the canes. Cut it out and fold it in half lengthways, with the fold on the right. Draw a line from the bottom left-hand corner, up to the top right-hand corner. Draw a line 1½ in (4 cm) long at right angles to the fold, where it meets the diagonal. Cut out the canvas along these lines.

Step 5

Using the shape you have just cut out as a template, cut out three more pieces on a single thickness of canvas, butting them as shown in the photograph so there is no waste.

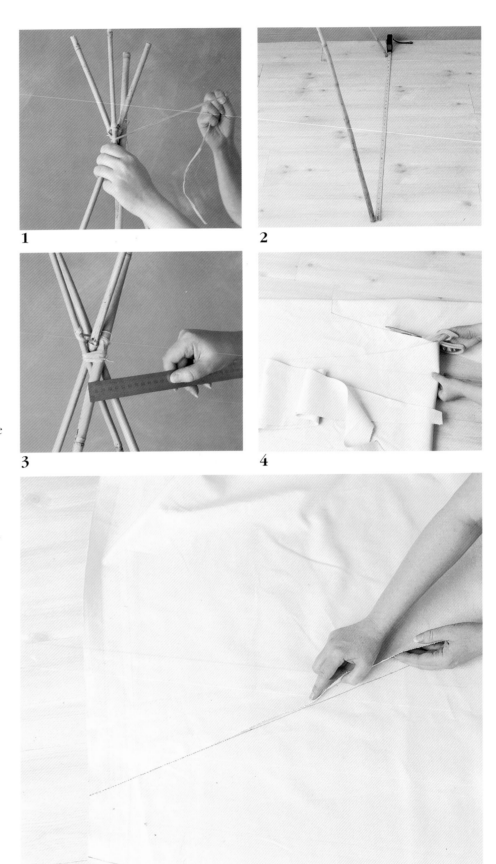

Step 6

To make an opening in the wigwam, take one of the triangles that you have just cut out, fold it in half and cut along the fold, about halfway up. Edge both sides of the opening with ribbon, pin and machine in place.

Step 7

To strengthen the top of the opening, cut a small square of canvas. Fray the edges by pulling at loose threads all the way round, then iron it onto the top of the opening with fusible web.

Day Two

Step 8

Pin and sew all the sides together. Then, to tie the wigwam to the canes, sew lengths of bias binding long enough to make a bow at three different points along the length of each seam. To do this, fold the bias binding ties in half, then pin them on the fold before machine sewing in place on the wrong side of the canvas.

Step 9

Press the seams flat with an iron. Edge the top and bottom of the wigwam with the same ribbon that you used to edge the opening.

Step 10

Place the finished wigwam over the stakes and adjust them so that they support the whole canvas. Tie the bias binding round the canes into bows, and let the children set up camp.

6

7

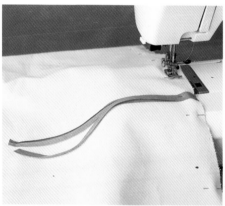

8

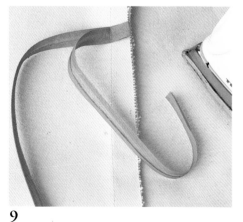

9

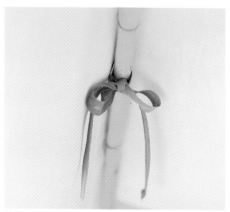

10

Wire frame for climbing plants

Twisted galvanized wire is a useful material. Made into a frame like this for climbing plants, it will make a focal point of any corner of the garden or patio.

Most seasonal climbing plants such as sweet peas, clematis or climbing nasturiums need some sort of support to grow up. Usually it is a fence, bamboo garden canes or trellis. This idea uses inexpensive and readily available materials to create a stunning effect.

Galvanized wire can be bought by the coil from building supply and DIY stores, and there is more than enough in one coil to make this frame. Twisting wire is quite a fiddly job and requires patience, and a friend to help. You need to slightly over-twist the wire so that it buckles a bit, but let it naturally unwind, slowly, and it will be straight. Once it is twisted, it is quite manageable and can be bent into many shapes with the aid of a pair of wire cutters or combination pliers. However, because it naturally formed a balloon shape, and fits well into this shape of plant pot, I left it like this. You could make right angles, and a variety of twists and turns if you wanted. Rocks from the garden, and a layer of gravel help to secure the wire in the bottom of the pot.

I pulled ivy from my garden wall where it was taking over, soaking it in a bucket to keep the stems pliable until I wove it around the wire. Just keep weaving pieces, adding several circles all around the frame. You can weave pieces around each other to make thicker or longer strands. Jasmine is also suitable for this kind of frame.

The frame is also ideal to support summer climbers, such as sweet peas, that are discarded at the end of the season, when the pot can be replanted.

Day One

Step 1

Begin by cutting six lengths of wire 3 yd (3 m) long. Twist two lengths together at a time, to give you three twisted lengths of 3 yd (3 m) each. Do this by bending each end around a scrap of wood; then one person holds their piece of wood still while the other twists. Twist until the wire straightens itself out and even begins to buckle. Let one end untwist itself slowly but be careful not to let go of the wire suddenly or it may fly up into your face and scratch you.

Step 2

Take one of the twisted lengths and bend it into a balloon shape. Put the two ends in the terracotta pot, anchoring one down first with rocks from the garden, then the other.

Step 3

Similarly bend the second and third lengths of wire and anchor them in the pot in the same way.

Step 4

Secure the center point where all the wires meet with a clothes pin, rearranging them to ensure they look equally spaced around the pot.

Step 5

To keep the wires together, tie them in place with a finer grade ⅟₁₆ in (1 mm) galvanized wire. Fill the pot half full with gravel to prevent the wires from moving around.

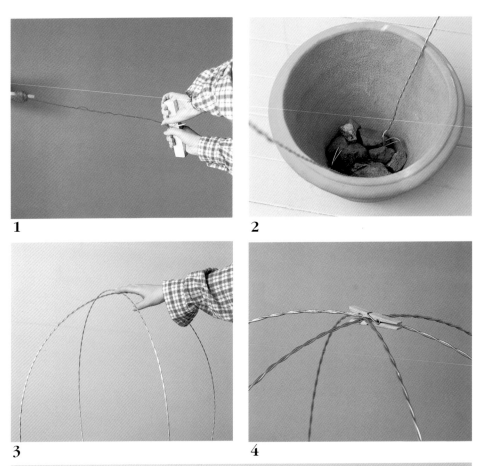

1

2

3

4

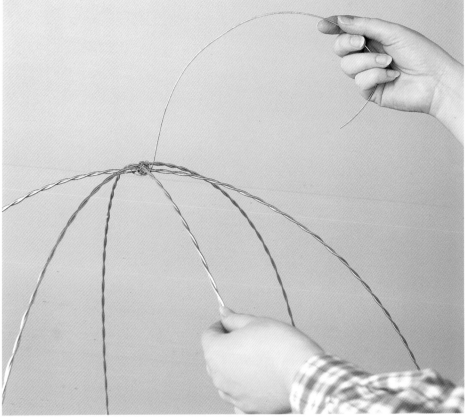

5

6

8

9

7

Step 6
Fill the pot with potting soil.

Step 7
Pull lengths of ivy from the fence or wall where it is unwanted and keep in a bucket of water to keep it pliable.

Day Two

Step 8
Take a long piece of ivy and cut off the longer roots and some of the leaves. Tie it with florists' wire onto each part of the twisted shape, until you have gone all the way round the frame in a circle. Continue until you have several rows, tying and weaving the ivy to the twisted wire as you go.

Step 9
For an all-year-round display, plant young variegated ivies and weave their stems around the wires as they grow.

Canopy

Long lunches on sunny summer afternoons are one of life's luxuries. This simple canopy will shade you and your guests from the heat of the midday sun.

Planning your time

DAY ONE
AM: Buy your materials and cut to size

PM: Attach screw eyes; make canvas canopy

DAY TWO
AM: Waterproof canvas; dig holes for poles

PM: Erect canopy

Tools and materials

Four 10 ft (3 m) rustic poles

4½ yd (4 m) of 15 oz (425 g) cotton duck canvas 72 in (183 cm) wide

Four 3 in (75 mm) eye screws

Four bottle screws

Four ⅝ in (15 mm) grommets

Eyelet cutting tool

Electric drill

6 ft (2 m) PVC pipe to fit the diameter of the rustic poles

Builders' sand or gravel

Wood scraps for wedges

Waterproof sealant for the canvas

Heavy-weight fusible web

A canopy always looks dramatic in a garden and this one is no exception, conjuring up romantic visions of Mediterranean evenings, Arabian tents and languid afternoons with plenty of wine and relaxed conversation!

This canopy is not meant to be a permanent fixture. It is designed to be taken down during the winter and also when it is windy. The idea is very simple – it consists of two widths of canvas that are sewn together and attached to four poles by means of eyelets and screws. The poles are young tree trunks still with their barks, so they have an attractive rustic appearance. Available from garden centers, they cost very little. To secure the poles in the ground, they are slipped into PVC rain pipes embedded into the ground, either in gravel and sand, or permanently cemented in.

Canvas is available from fine arts and crafts stores, fabric stores or boat builders', and on this occasion I have weatherproofed it, although canvas will repel water to a certain extent. If there is a downpour you should take the canopy down anyway, because it will become extremely heavy.

Instead of canvas you could also use an old dyed sheet or curtain fabric. For a dreamy look sew lengths of voile together.

Day One

Step 1

Drill pilot holes for the eye screws about 8 in (20 cm) from the top of each pole. Screw in each eye screw so that it is at a right angle to the pole.

Step 2

Cut off a narrow strip of canvas for strengthening the corners. Cut the remaining canvas in half, so that you have two pieces just under 6 ft (2 m) long. Join them together with an overlapped seam and two lines of stitching. To get the canvas through the machine, roll the excess up and push it through the center of the machine as you sew.

Step 3

Two lines of stitching will make a stronger seam. Reverse the stitching for about 2 in (5 cm) to finish the ends. Stop the seam some ¾ in (2 cm) short of the edge of the canvas.

Step 4

Fray the edges of the canvas to give a soft edge.

Step 5

Cut four 3¼ in (8 cm) squares of canvas from the narrow strip that you have already cut off. Fray the edges and attach onto each corner with fusible web, using a hot iron.

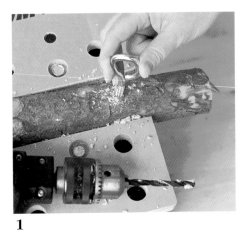

1

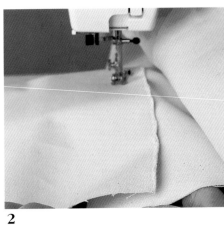

2

3

4

5

6

7

8

9

10

Step 6

Bang a grommet into each corner. The cutting tool may not go through all the thicknesses, so you may need to snip at the hole with a sharp pair of scissors or x-acto knife.

Day Two

Step 7

To waterproof the canopy, lay the canvas out on the ground and paint on a waterproof sealant.

Step 8

While the canvas is drying, cut the PVC pipe into four pieces. Dig four holes where the canopy is to be located, 8 in (20 cm) smaller all round than the size of the canvas. The holes need to be slightly bigger than the pipe. At least half the pipe should be in the ground.

Step 9

Fill the space around the pipe with sand or gravel so that it fits tightly into the ground. If the pipe wobbles, hammer some wedges in around it.

Step 10

Slide the poles into the pipes. If they are a bit tight, shave the ends carefully.

Step 11

Attach the canopy to the poles, using bottle screws. It will take two people to do this as the canopy is very heavy.

11

Mosaic pond

*If you only have a balcony, patio or the smallest
of gardens, you still have room for a pond.
Mosaics are fashionable and this pond provides
a welcome oasis in a busy world.*

Inspired by Japanese ornamental
pools, to bring a little tranquillity
to modern life, this freestanding
pond will be a calming factor in
any setting. The cool blue of the tiles
promotes restfulness and is set off by
colorful waterlilies. You can lose hours
in contemplation just watching the
water and the fish.

Mosaic tiles are quite expensive to
buy, so work out the size of your pond
and your requirements before you go
off to buy them; you can order them
from swimming-pool suppliers. Make
all your dimensions divisible by the
size of a tile, including the thickness of the walls of the pond.

The carcass is made from marine plywood, which has waterproof qualities.
All the joins are sealed with PVA glue and screwed in place, so the pond is
secure. Make sure you use swimming-pool adhesive, which is available from
speciality shops (unfortunately, it only seems to be available in huge bags). You
can buy waterproof grout at a building supply store.

I bought four 4 in (10 cm) square sets from a garden center that stocks
stones for building driveways, to stand the pond on to keep it off the ground.

Planning your time

DAY ONE
AM: Buy the materials

PM: Construct the frame; tile
inside and out

DAY TWO
AM: Grout the tiles; fix and paint
the beading

PM: When grout has dried fill up
with water

Tools and materials

⅝ in (15 mm) marine plywood

Mosaic tiles (tesserae)

Beading

Waterproof PVA glue

Swimming-pool adhesive

Swimming-pool grout

4 x 4 in (10 x 10 cm) square sets

1

2

3

Day One

Step 1

Mosaic tiles are supplied on a mesh backing. Measure the size of a sheet of tiles and decide on the internal measurements of the pond in proportion to the size of sheet that is available.

Step 2

Cut the structure of the pond from ⅝ in (15 mm) thick marine plywood, using a jigsaw with a fine blade.

Step 3

To make the pond you need to cut a base, four sides and four "lip" pieces for a rim at the top of the pond.

Step 4

Plywood tends to splinter when you cut it, so sand the edges smooth.

4

5

6

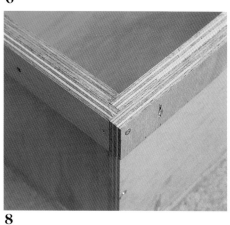

7

8

Step 5
Place the sides at right angles to each other, then drill pilot holes through the thickness of the first piece and into the width of the second.

Step 6
Glue each piece with a waterproof PVA glue and screw together through the pilot holes that you have drilled.

Step 7
Glue and screw the base to the sides.

Step 8
Glue and screw the lip pieces to the top edge of the pond, overlapping them to add strength to the structure as shown in the photograph.

Step 9
Make sure that the tiles fit before you start to mix up the adhesive, so that you will not make any mistakes when you start to stick them to the inside of the pond.

9

Filling the pond

Fill the pond with water using a hose when the grouting is completely dry (see Step 17). Check with pond suppliers on the number of fish suitable for the size of your pond and add oxygenating plants to keep the water clear.

10

11

12

Step 10

The tesserae I used are a standard blue mix. To add random contrast colors or highlights, pick out a few tiles here and there on each sheet of tiles.

Step 11

Mix up the adhesive in a bowl, following the manufacturer's instructions. Wear rubber gloves to protect your hands.

Step 12

Spread the adhesive on the base of the pond and lay the tiles, inserting the contrast tiles. To get them to lay flat, press them down into the adhesive with a scrap of wood.

Step 13

Continue spreading the adhesive sparingly, using a tile spreader, along the sides.

13

16

17

14

15

Step 14

Apply the tesserae to the sides of the pond, pressing them flat with your hands. When you have tiled the pond inside and out and added a line of tiles across the top edge, leave to dry.

Day Two

Step 15

Mix up the grout and apply with a sponge, following the manufacturer's instructions. Leave to dry.

Step 16

Cut the beading to fit around the top edge of the pond, alongside the single line of tiles. Use a mitre block to obtain a 45-degree angle.

Step 17

Glue and tack the beading in place. Paint with a wood stain and fill in any gaps with waterproof grout.

Decking

This decking is ideal for terraces, roof gardens, or grassed areas where you do not want a permanent patio. Because it is portable it can also be useful for rented apartments and summer cottages.

These adaptable squares of decking will add an extra dimension to your garden. They can turn a shady corner into a focal point or can even be used in the middle of the lawn for a special occasion, where you might want to save the grass, or where there are a few bald patches.

The ones I made are 20 in (50 cm) square, and are constructed like small pallets but from planed lumber. I made thirty altogether, giving 9 sq yd (7.5 square meters), but you can make as many as you need for a given area. I painted these with a water-based exterior wood stain, which was touch dry in about thirty minutes, so the decking could be handled quite quickly after painting. You could use acrylic paint, but varnish afterwards with an exterior varnish; or even use an exterior gloss paint, though this will take considerably longer to dry.

I chose three complementary colors for the decking, to create interest. They could be laid in stripes of color, or diagonally as here. These pale ice-cream colors are classic summer tones and bring a touch of glamor to a garden, roof terrace or balcony. You can even use them indoors in a conservatory!

Planning your time

DAY ONE
AM: Buy your materials; cut out all the pieces

PM: Paint with wood stain

DAY TWO
AM: Drill holes in the smaller pieces; join together

PM: Lay the decking

Tools and materials

6 x ¾ in (150 x 20 mm) pine

35 x 35 mm (1¼ x 1¼ in) pine or spruce

Three different color exterior wood stains

Galvanized screws

Sandpaper and sanding block

Vice

Jigsaw

Electric drill

Day One

Step 1

To make a 20 in (50 cm) square piece of decking, as I did, measure out three 20 in (50 cm) lengths of 6 x ¾ in (150 x 20 mm) pine and three 20 in (50 cm) lengths of 1¼ x 1¼ in (35 x 35 mm) pine.

Step 2

Put each piece in a vice to hold it steady and cut with a jigsaw, moving each length along so that the point where you cut it is held as tightly in the vice as possible.

Step 3

You should now have six equal lengths of wood, three to make the top, and three to make the bottom supports.

Step 4

Sand the ends smooth with a medium-grade sandpaper wrapped around a cork block; a kitchen matchbox will suffice if you do not have a cork block.

Step 5

Rest the pieces for the decking on scraps of wood and paint them all on both sides and edges with an exterior colored wood stain. The one I used is water-based so does not take long to dry.

   Repeat the above process until you have cut and painted as many pieces as you need.

1

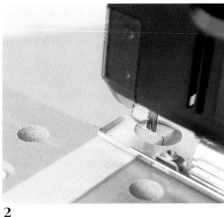

2

3

4

5

Using a jigsaw safely

Always use a vice when cutting wood with a jigsaw. It keeps the wood steady and reduces the likelihood of an accident. Always make sure the jigsaw cable is safely behind the direction in which you are cutting.

Day Two

Step 6

Roughly lay out the decking in the position it will be joined together, but upside down. Mark and drill six countersunk holes in each of the three pieces of $1\frac{1}{4}$ x $1\frac{1}{4}$ in (35 x 35 mm) pine, to correspond with the position of the wider top pieces underneath. When you have done this, screw down the front top piece, making sure that the corners are square.

Step 7

Screw down the back top piece in place.

Step 8

Screw on the opposite underside.

Step 9

Lay the last top piece in the center and screw through the drilled holes into the back, then place the last underside piece in the middle and screw this to the top piece.

Step 10

Turn the square of decking the right way up. Make another twenty-nine and you have got yourself a patio!

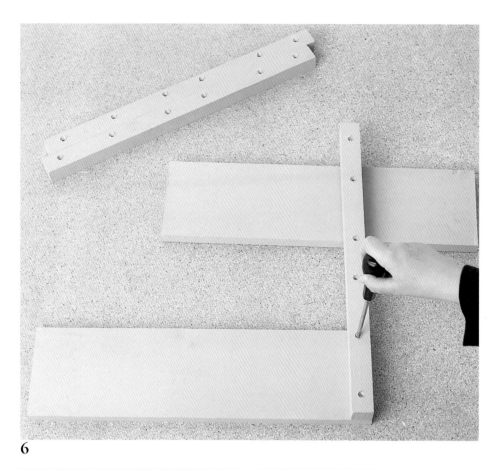

6

7

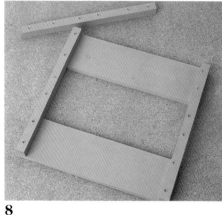

8

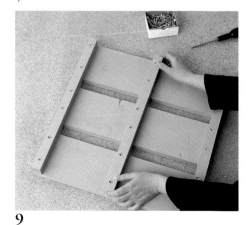

9

10

Glossary

Bradawl

Flat wood drill bit

Mitre box

Batten
A strip of sawed lumber that is usually 7 inches wide, less than 4 inches thick, and more than 6 feet long; usually used for flooring.

Bias binding
Strips of fabric that are cut across the weave (bias) of a fabric, which gives it flexibility so that it can be used on corners and curves easily.

Bottle screws
Sometimes called link screws. The link has a screw that locks completely, like on a keyring, making a complete link.

Bradawl
A tool used to make a small hole in wood before fixing panel pins or screws—the starter hole helps prevent the wood from splitting.

Copper clout nails
Copper nails with a big head, so they are easier to hit. Made of copper, they will not rust.

Cotton duck canvas
Unbleached 100 per cent cotton canvas cloth available in different weights, 10 oz (285 g), 12 oz (340 g), 15 oz (425 g) etc. It is slightly water resistant; water will form beads on its surface.

Countersinking tool
A drill attachment that drills a pilot hole through two pieces of wood, and allows the head of the screw to sit below the level of the wood.

PVC pipe
Plastic pipe of differing diameters and length used for drainpipes.

Eyelet punch
A plier that presses the eyelet components together. Used instead of a hammer on small eyelets.

Fabric paint
Paint specifically for use on fabric, for stencilling, freehand painting or stamping. Must be sealed with a hot iron to make it washproof.

Flat wood drill bit
A flat blade-like drill bit with a pointed end for drilling large holes in wood. The point makes a pilot hole for the flat blade.

Former
A shape or arc on which to bend lengths of tubing without flattening them.

Florists' wire
Soft pliable wire used by florists in flower arranging, but also useful for joining lengths of wire together. Similar to fuse wire.

Fusible Web
A filmy bonding strip that allows two fabrics to be fused together with a hot iron. Brand names include Wonder-Web and Stitch Witchery.

Galvanized wire
Wire treated with zinc to make it rustproof.

Lead-free solder
Used by plumbers to make joins in pipes watertight. It is very pliable.

Miter box
Using a mitre box in conjunction with a saw enables 45° angle cutting of wood so that the butted pieces make a right angle.

Mosaic tesserae
Small pieces of tile made out of stone, glass or ceramic. They are set into a cement to create a decorative and hard-wearing surface.

Nippers
Used to cut mosaic tiles.

Planed softwood
Pine or spruce wood that has had the bark removed and planed smooth in usable sizes. The sizes given in shops or building supply stores are unplaned sizes, just to confuse you.

PVA glue
A white water-based glue that dries clear and gives a strong bond. EVA is the outdoor equivalent.

Resist outliner
Used for silk painting to provide a barrier for paint and can also be used on other fabrics to make a relief pattern. Comes in a tube with a small pointed nozzle for drawing fine lines. Available from craft shops.

Round-nosed pliers
Pliers with round instead of flat ends that will bend wire without flattening it.

Rustic poles
Young felled trees with their bark left on, available from most good garden centers.

Mosaic tesserae

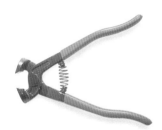

Nippers

Round-nosed pliers

Sandpaper

Sandpaper
Also known as glasspaper,
sandpaper is available in various
grades from very fine, for finishing
work, to coarse grade or grit for
heavier work.

Sawn lumber
Softwood that is left unplaned and
is rough. Mainly used outdoors and
is sometimes pressure treated to
prevent rotting.

Screw eyes
Screws with a loop on the end
instead of a head, for hanging things
from. Available in different sizes.

Softwood
Lumber from coniferous trees such
as pine, cedar, fir, hemlock, spruce,
cypress, and redwood.

Spring former
A tube of coiled wire that can be
slipped into pipes so that the pipe
can be bent without flattening it.

Swimming-pool adhesive
Specially formulated adhesive that
will stand up to the elements and
extremes of temperature.

Tenon saw
A short fine-toothed saw. If you are
buying a new saw, choose one that
is as long as possible as this will
give you a longer sweep with each
cut and the work will be faster.

Waterproof grout
Grout that is suitable for total
immersion in water, such as in
swimming pools. Most grout in DIY
stores is not waterproof, so look for
it in a building supply store.

Wire cutters
Will cut different grades of wire.
Combination pliers will do the
same job.

Wood stain
A wood stain allows the grain of the
wood to show through and actually
penetrates the surface to offer the
wood protection against the
elements.

Tenon saw

Wire cutters

Suppliers

2000 Art Supplies
www.2000-art.com
Extensive selection of acrylic, oil, watercolor, and ceramic paints, canvas, brushes and more. On-line catalog.

All Seasons Company
www.allseasons.com
888 Brannan #1160
San Francisco, CA 94103
Tel. 415-864-3308
Fax. 415-864-5001
Beads, sequins, rhinestones, diamantes, jeweler's wire, adhesives, findings.

Artglass
www.artglass-source.com
Tel. 518-371-0977
Fax. 518-371-9423
Tiles, grout, cutters, adhesives and supplies for mosaic work.

Ben Franklin Crafts
www.benfranklinstores.com
Nationwide chain of crafts stores; extensive selection of stenciling, decoupage, gilding, stamping and painting supplies. Web site provides directory of stores.

Crafter's Components Catalog
www.lamp-specialties.com
Tel. 800-CALL-LAMP
Complete resources for crafters including ceramic work, frame blanks, paints, beads, mosaics, brushes and more.

Dover Publications
31 East 2nd Street
Mineola, NY 11501
Tel. 516-294-7000
Fax. 516-742-5049
Extensive selection of art books containing copyright-free lithographs, typography sets, frames, borders and other images for decoupage, transfer and other design work.

Effie Glitzfinger's St. Louis Stamp Design
www.glitzfinger.com
12906 Barbezieus Drive
St. Louis, MO 63141
Tel. 800-450-8586
Fax. 800-450-0185
Templates, brushes, paints, suplies for stenciling projects.

Fascinating Folds
www.fascinating-folds.com
P.O. Box 10070
Glendale, AZ 85318
Tel. 800-968-2418
Supplies for decoupage, quilling, parchment and other paper craft, including embossing metals, florist foils, reproduction documents, vintage nautical maps and more.

Faux Like A Pro
www.fauxlikeapro.com
Tel. 617-713-4320
Complete line of paints, glazes, brushes, tools and accessories for faux-finish painting.

Lee Valley & Veritas
www.leevalley.com
Fine woodworking and Gardening Tools
P.O. Box 1780
Ogdensburg, NY 13669
Tel. 800-871-8158
Fax. 800-513-7885
Fine woodworking tools, fittings, and supplies, garden supplies and furnishings.

Mosaic Mercantile
www.mosaicmerc.com
Wholesale supplier of tiles, grout, ceramic paint, and tools. $250 minimum order. On-line search engine lists retail outlets.

Nancy's Notions
www.nancysnotions.com
333 Beichl Avenue
P.O. Box 683
Beaver Dam WI 53916
Fusible web, quilter's tape, sewing accessories and notions for sewing.

Staedtler, Inc.
21900 Plummer Street
Chatsworth, CA 91311
Tel. 800-800-3691
Fax. 800-675-8249
Watercolor pan sets, brushes, markers, calligraphy pens.

Stencil-Ease
www.stencilease.com
P.O. Box 1127
Old Saybrook, CT 06475
Tel. 860-395-0150
Fax. 860-395-0166
Complete assortment of brushes, stencils, templates, paints and stenciling supplies.

Woodtown Unfinished Furniture
www.woodtownusa.com
13951 Riverview Drive
Elk River, MN 55330
Tel./Fax 800-510-WOOD
On-line catalog of unfinished furniture and accessories.

Uhlfelder Gold Leaf
www.uhlfeldergoldleaf.com
420 South Fulton Avenue
Mount Vernon, NY 10553
Tel. 800-664-LUCO
Fax. 914-664-8721
High quality gold leaf and other gilding and art supplies.

USArtQuest, Inc.
www.usartquest.com
Tel. 800-200-7848
Fax. 517-522-6225
Art brushes, paints, canvas, art paper, supplies.

Index

A
adhesive, tile, 70
arbor, copper, 12–17

B
bamboo canes, wigwam, 54, 56
basket, hanging, 34–7
battens, stepping stones, 46–7
bird house, 28–33
bolsters, 38, 42–3

C
canopy, 62–5
canvas:
  canopy, 62–5
  children's wigwam, 54–7
  tablecloth, 50–3
cement:
  mixing, 47–8
  stepping stones, 44–9
chicken wire, hanging basket, 34–7
children's wigwam, 54–7
climbing plants, wire frame for, 58–61
copper arbor, 12–17

D
decking, 72–5

E
étagère, 22–7
eyelets:
  canopy, 65
  mattress cover, 42
  tablecloth, 50, 53

F
fabric:
  canopy, 62–5
  children's wigwam, 54–7
  eyelets, 42
  joining seams without sewing, 41
  mattress cover, 40–3
  tablecloth, 50–3
fabric paint:
  tablecloth, 50–3
  watering down, 52

foam mattress, 38–43
formers, 15
furniture:
  games table, 8–11
  pallet sun lounger, 38–43
fusible web:
  bolster cover, 43
  canopy, 64
  mattress cover, 41
  tablecloth, 50

G
galvanized wire, frame for climbing plants, 58–61
games table, 8–11
glass jar night lights, 18–19, 21
grout, mosaic pond, 71

H
hanging basket, 34–7

J
jars, night lights, 18–19, 21
jigsaws, 31, 74

L
lead-free solder, stepping stones, 49
lights, night, 18–21

M
marine plywood, mosaic pond, 66–9
mattress, foam, 38–43
mosaic:
  mosaic pond, 66–71
  stepping stones, 49

N
night lights, 18–21

P
paint:
  canopy, 65
  economies, 10
  fabric paint, 52
  tablecloth, 50–3
pallet sun lounger, 38–43

paving slabs, stepping stones, 44–9
pebbles:
  hanging basket, 37
  tablecloth, 50, 53
pipes:
  copper arbor, 12–17
plants:
  mosaic pond, 69
  wire frame for climbing plants, 58–61
plywood, mosaic pond, 66–9
pond, mosaic, 66–71

R
rustic poles, canopy, 65

S
safety, jigsaws, 74
saws, jigsaws, 31, 74
seams, joining without sewing, 41
solder, stepping stones, 49
spring formers, 15
staging, étagère, 22–7
stepping stones, 44–9
storage, étagère, 22–7
sun lounger, 38–43

T
table, games, 8–11
tablecloth, 50–3
tesserae, mosaic pond, 70–1
tiles, mosaic pond, 66–71
tin can night lights, 18–20

W
wigwam, children's, 54–7
wire:
  frame for climbing plants, 58–61
  hanging basket, 34–7
  stepping stones, 44, 49
wood:
  bird house, 28–33
  decking, 72–5
  étagère, 22–7
  games table, 8–11
  pallet sun lounger, 38–43